MW01643791

BIOENERGY

GRAHAM HOUGHTON

Gareth Stevens Children's Books
MILWAUKEE

Titles in the Alternative Energy series:

Bioenergy
Geothermal Energy
Solar Energy
Water Energy
Wind Energy

For a free color catalog describing Gareth Stevens' list of high-quality books, call 1-800-542-2595 (USA) or 1-800-461-9120 (Canada). Gareth Stevens' Fax: (414) 225-0377.

Library of Congress Cataloging-in-Publication Data

Houghton, Graham, 1950-
Bioenergy / Graham Houghton.
p. cm. — (Alternative energy)
"First published in the United Kingdom, copyright 1990, by Wayland (Publishers) Limited"—T.p. verso.
Includes index.
Summary: Describes the various kinds of bioenergy, ways we are using it today, and its advantages and disadvantages.
ISBN 0-8368-0707-3
1. Biomass energy—Juvenile literature. [1. Biomass energy.] I. Title. II. Series: Alternative energy (Milwaukee, Wis.)
TP360.H68 1991
662'.88—dc20 91-9259

North American edition first published in 1991 by

Gareth Stevens Publishing
1555 North RiverCenter Drive, Suite 201
Milwaukee, Wisconsin 53212, USA

Picture acknowledgements

Artwork by Nick Hawken

The publishers would like to thank the following for supplying photographs: David Bowden, 12; Energy Technology Support Unit, 26; Environmental Picture Library, cover, 6, 11, 24; Eye Ubiquitous, 9; Geoscience Features, 23; Hutchison, 4, 19, 21, 25; Christine Osborne, 10; Photri, 8, 16; Topham/Associated Press, 14, 17; Zefa, 7, 13, 22.

Editors (UK): Paul Mason and William Wharfe
Editor (U.S.): Eileen Foran
Designers: Charles Harford and David Armitage
Consultant: Mike Flood, Ph.D.

Printed in the United States of America

3 4 5 6 7 8 9 99 98 97

Contents

Words that appear in the glossary are printed in **boldface** type the first time they appear in the text.

WHY ALTERNATIVE ENERGY?

Most of the energy we use is produced by burning **fossil fuels**, such as coal, oil, and natural gas. These fuels formed millions of years ago out of the remains of dead plants and animals.

Fossil fuels take millions of years to develop. In the past 200 years or so, we have used up what was once an abundance of fossil fuel. The day will come when the last piece of coal is burned and the last drop of gasoline is put into a gas tank. Our homes could then grow cold. Our factories could stop working. And our transportation could grind to a halt.

Cars that use gasoline, such as these on a busy highway in California, are using a resource we cannot replace.

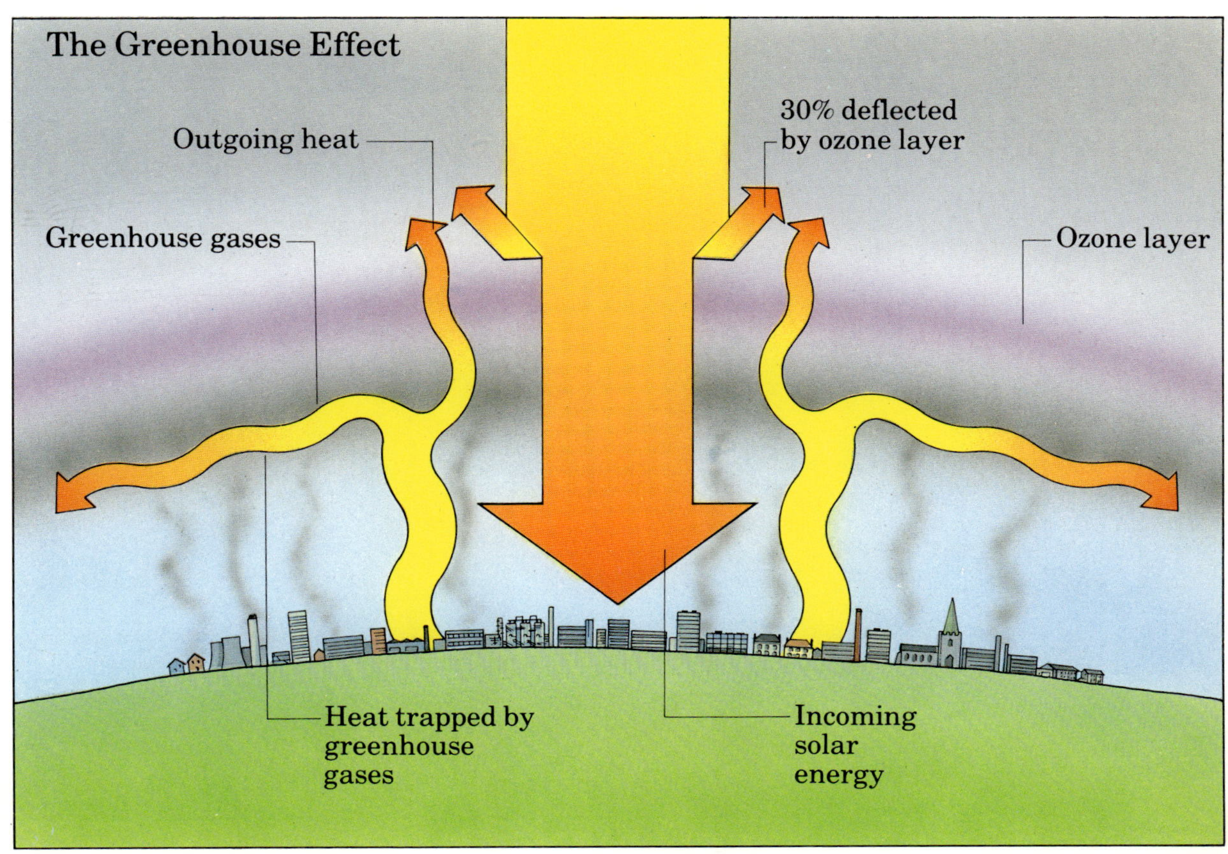

*The use of fossil fuels causes the **greenhouse effect**, which will probably lead to warmer weather. The greenhouse effect may cause flooding in low-lying areas and drought in warm countries.*

With oil, that day might come as soon as the year 2020! This is not so surprising when you realize that California alone uses about a billion gallons (3.8 billion L) of gasoline each month, or that more coal has been burned since World War II than in all the time before then. The demand for coal grows greater every day, and it is being consumed at an alarming rate.

Burning fossil fuels creates serious **pollution**. When things burn, they release gases into the air. Some of these gases are called **greenhouse gases** because they keep in the Sun's heat, much as the glass in a greenhouse does.

Most of the energy coming from the Sun that reaches the Earth escapes back into space. Some of the Sun's energy, however, is trapped by the greenhouse gases in the air. These gases stay in our atmosphere and keep our planet warm enough to live on.

*One effect of burning fossil fuel is **acid rain**, which kills trees and fish and pollutes lakes and forests.*

But by burning fossil fuel, we are actually increasing the amount of greenhouse gases in the air. More heat is being trapped and the Earth is becoming warmer.

This may sound like a good thing, but a change in the climate will do more harm than good. For instance, there may be crop failures due to lack of rain, and sea levels may rise as ice melts at the North and South poles.

Other gases, such as carbon dioxide and **methane**, are released by burning fossil fuels. These gases dissolve in rain as it falls to the ground and turn the rain into a strong acid. Lakes and forests in

A family in North Africa begins the day with tea warmed over a wood fire. This has been done for centuries.

years, giving people the right to go into forests to collect firewood.

Making **charcoal** from wood was among the earliest methods of converting biomass into a more **efficient** fuel. It is an important industry in many developing countries today. Charcoal produces twice the heat of wood.

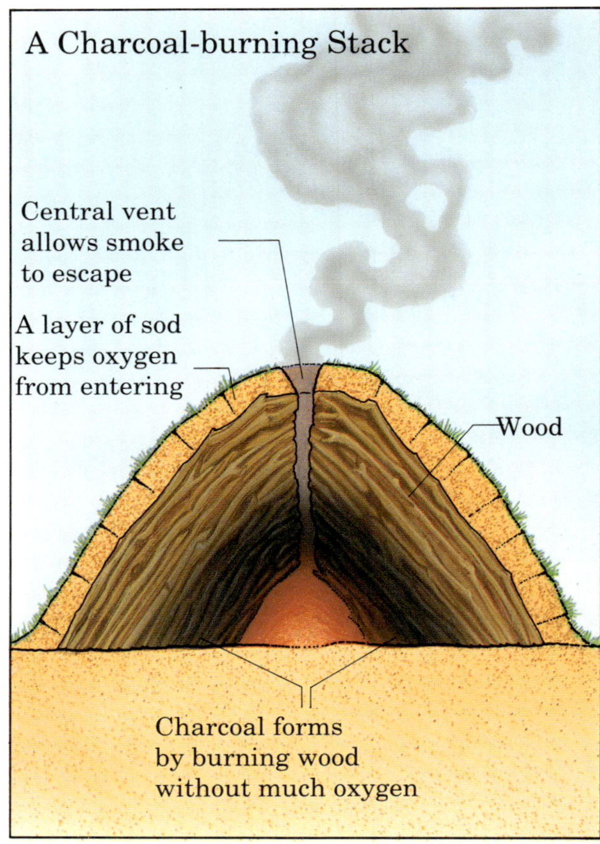

Above: Charcoal burning has been an important way of using biofuel in many parts of the world for centuries.

Charcoal is made by burning wood without much air. This can be done by building a pile of logs and branches so that a natural chimney is formed through the center. This pile is then covered with tightly packed earth, and a fire is then lit underneath. Once the pile is burning properly, the air holes are blocked and it is left to burn for two to three days. After the pile burns for a few days, charcoal is made.

Years ago, wood and charcoal were used to fuel kilns in which pottery was made. Charcoal was used to **smelt** ores that produced metal. Bread ovens were heated by burning piles of wood in them. Then, the ashes were cleaned out and the bread put in to bake.

Blacksmiths used large amounts of charcoal to make tools,

Below: This man in China is making charcoal bricks to use as fuel.

Blacksmiths have always used wood, coal, or charcoal to provide themselves with temperatures high enough to melt metal.

weapons, and armor. This fuel remained important in Western nations until the beginning of the Industrial Revolution, when the earliest steam engines were powered by wood-fired boilers, which replaced the charcoal-powered engines.

Biofuel is still an important energy source in many countries. In the last 200 years or so, however, the industrialized world has depended more heavily on fossil fuels and has not fully used biofuel as the efficient and useful energy source that it is.

RELEASING BIOENERGY

Biofuels come in many forms. Wood, coconut shells, straw, rice husks, sugarcane, and even dried animal dung are all biofuels.

The easiest way of releasing the energy contained in such materials is to set them on fire. This has been the traditional way of using biofuels for hundreds of thousands of years.

These fuels do have some disadvantages, though. First, collecting the materials takes up a lot of time. Second, large, dry storage areas must be built to keep them in. Third, burning biofuels in the open wastes a lot of energy. Most of the heat produced by an open fire escapes before it can heat anything.

You can better understand why open fires are inefficient by learning how a fire burns in a traditional fireplace. Coal and wood are the fuels that are usually burned. As the fuel burns, it spreads heat into the room, causing the air in the room to warm. But this same warm air

Biofuels can be a source of fun as well as a useful source of needed energy. Bonfires such as this one in Sweden are common throughout the world.

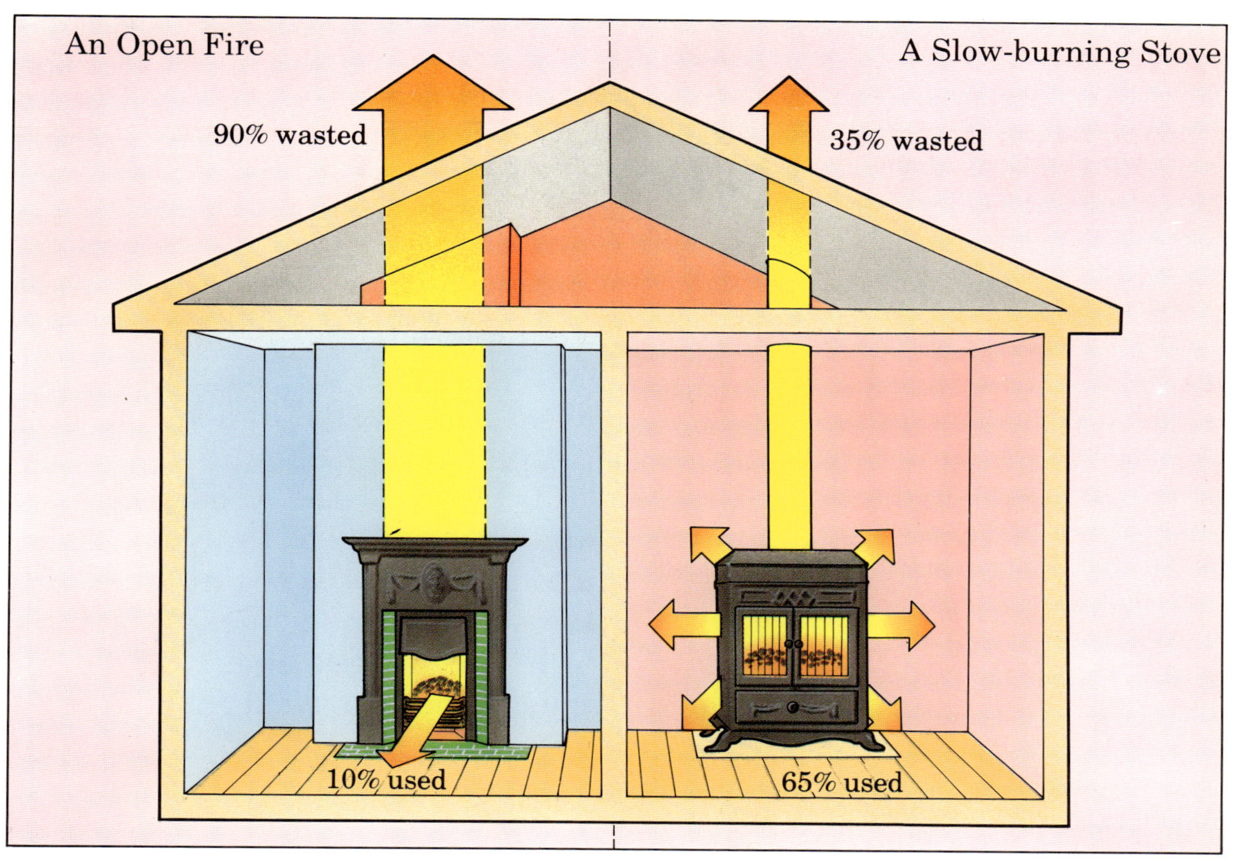

Open fires waste a lot more heat than do sealed stoves. Most of their energy goes up the chimney.

supplies the oxygen to keep the fire burning. So the warm air is drawn from the room, into the fire, and then up the chimney. It must then be replaced.

The warm air is replaced by cold air, drawn from outside the building through gaps in windows and doors. In this way, cold drafts are created. More fuel must be burned to warm the cold air that has been drawn into the room.

Sealed slow-combustion stoves keep much of the heat from escaping up the chimney. Vents can be opened and closed to control the amount of air taken in. Slow-combustion stoves waste less warm air than ordinary fires. Because of this, they need less fuel to heat a room.

The first successful stove of this type was built in the United States in 1836. Modern sealed stoves not only provide room heating, but can also supply hot water for radiators and washing. Many also have a built-in oven and surface for cooking.

BIOMASS INTO OTHER FUELS

Biomass can be converted into four different fuels. The first is charcoal (see pages 11-13), an ancient fuel. The other basic types of biofuel are roasted wood, natural gas, and **gasohol**, a liquid fuel similar to gasoline.

Roasted wood

Roasted wood is an alternative to charcoal. Roasted wood is made by chopping logs into chips about two inches (5 cm) long. These are dried and roasted in a kiln at a temperature of about 570°F (300°C). Roasted wood is cleaner and more efficient than charcoal, and thus reduces the number of trees cut down for fuel. A factory in France makes about 10,000 tons of roasted wood each year.

Most of the trees these lumberjacks are cutting will be used for building, but they may also be used as an alternative fuel source.

Biogas from roasted wood

The production of roasted wood yields **biogas**. If the temperature in the kiln rises to about 2,700°F (1,500°C) and oxygen is pumped in, large amounts of biogas are produced. This gas is then used to power engines that in turn power electric generators. This process, called **gasification**, is not new. Gasoline and diesel fuel were difficult to obtain during World War II, so many trucks were converted to run on gas produced from biofuels. Some even had their own biogas generators built onto them. In addition to having an exhaust system from the engine, they had a tall, smoking chimney.

The wood chips that are used to make roasted wood.

Harold Bate, a British inventor who runs his car on biogas.

Biogas from waste

Biogas can also be made from materials such as sewage and waste. Bacteria decompose these **organic** materials and produce gases such as methane. Methane is **flammable** and can be used as a fuel. In order for bacteria to decompose organic materials and produce methane, they must be kept in a warm, airless environment.

Biogas **digesters** are designed to promote an environment that will produce methane. A digester is a tank into which sewage or sorted garbage is pumped. After the compost is pumped into the tank, it might need to be heated to the correct temperature, or the gas-producing bacteria may need to be put into the tank.

The bacteria digest the waste, emitting methane in the process. The methane is then carried through pipes to another tank or a giant plastic balloon, where the methane is stored. This gas is used to power generators that produce electricity. An additional benefit of producing biogas from sewage and waste is that the solid waste left behind in the digester makes an excellent fertilizer for food crops. Biogas digesters are already an important source of energy in a number of countries. Biogas digesters are particularly useful in small farming communities, where large amounts of animal dung and other organic wastes are available, and are suitable for just such a purpose. India and China were among the first countries to build small-scale biogas digesters.

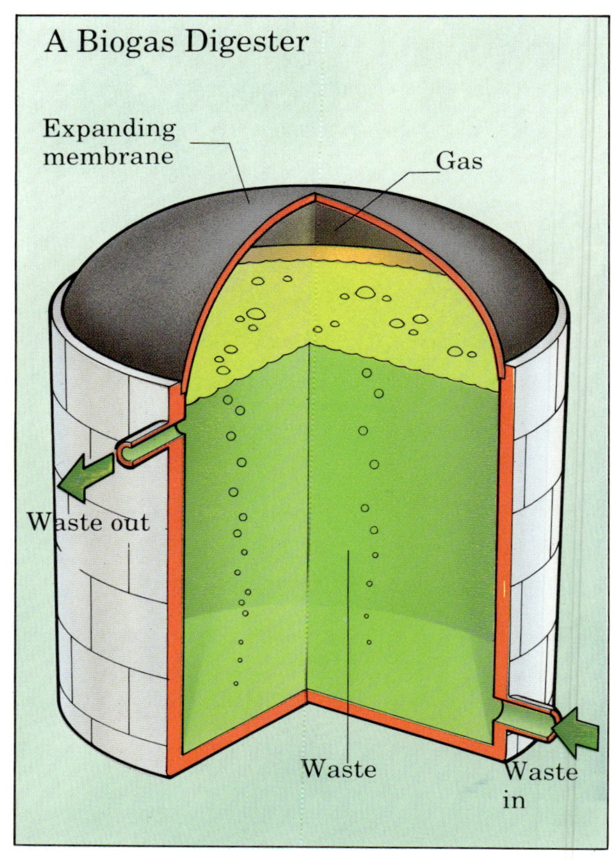

One type of small-scale biogas digester. There are many others.

This biogas digester produces methane gas from cow manure. The gas provides a farm with energy.

China has some 4.5 million working digesters. India has about 30 large-scale plants and thousands of small plants supplying energy to large communities across the country.

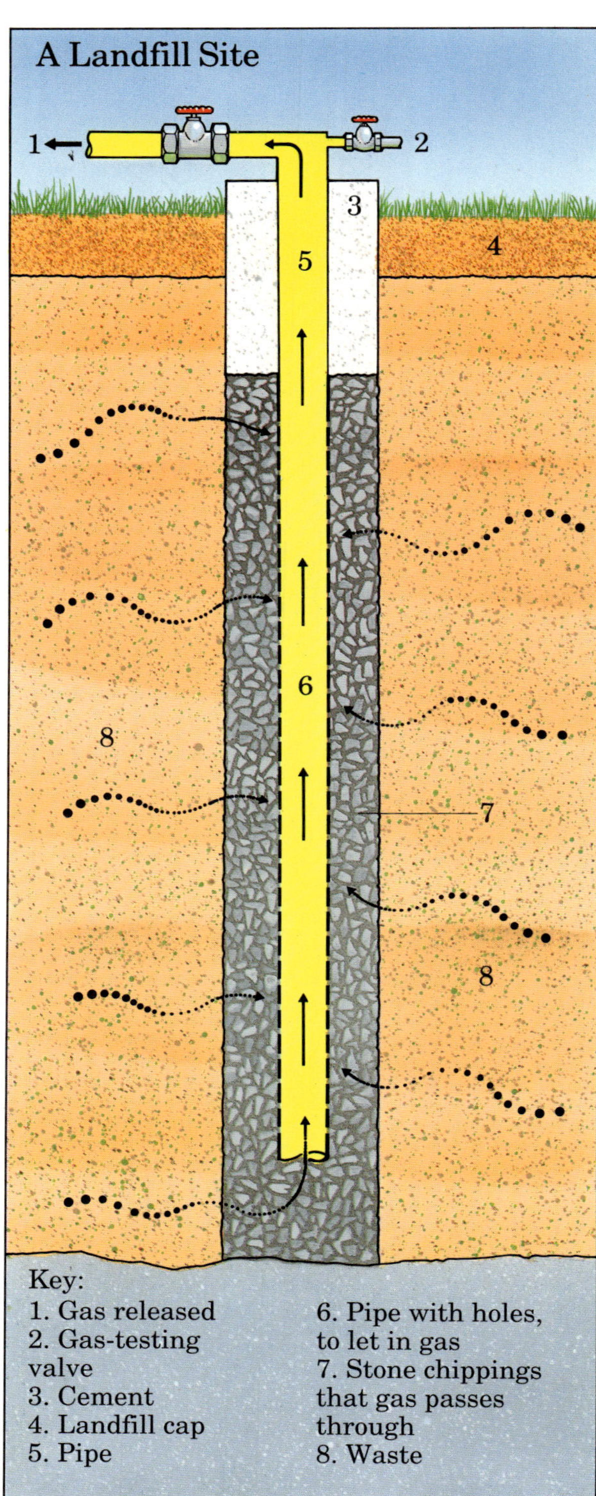

Biogas is also produced in large amounts at public landfill sites. Large holes in the ground are filled with waste. These sites receive large amounts of household and industrial garbage every day. When the sites are full, they are sealed with earth and clay. The methane that forms as the garbage decays is trapped underground.

Engineers drill into large landfill sites to remove this methane, which is potentially hazardous because it could explode if kept trapped and sealed underground. This methane is sold to factories, which have many uses for it. The first site to sell its methane was in Palos Verdes, California, where the gas was used to power electric generators. Now there are over 80 landfill sites in the United States producing methane. Other countries are following. In Britain, for example, bricks are fired in kilns fueled with landfill gas. Large diesel engines use methane from the same landfill site to power generators that supply electricity to nearby homes.

Left: A landfill site.

Although Britain has fewer landfill sites than the United States supplying methane gas, the number is increasing.

A landfill site in England. After it has been covered and methane has built up under the surface, it will be possible to use the gas as fuel.

Running cars on biofuel

Liquid fuel can be made from biomass with a high sugar content. Liquid fuel is made by fermenting it to produce alcohol. **Fermentation** occurs when yeasts digest sugar and make alcohol as a waste product. Beer and wine are made through fermentation. The sugar used in fermentation comes from plants like sugarcane, sugar beets, and grains, wood, and even seaweed. After harvest, the sugar is squeezed from these plants, usually by crushing them. Yeast is added to the sugar solution. In a few days, the sugar is converted to alcohol. The alcohol is then removed from the sugar solution.

Above: A car in Brazil being filled with "alcool," a form of gasohol.

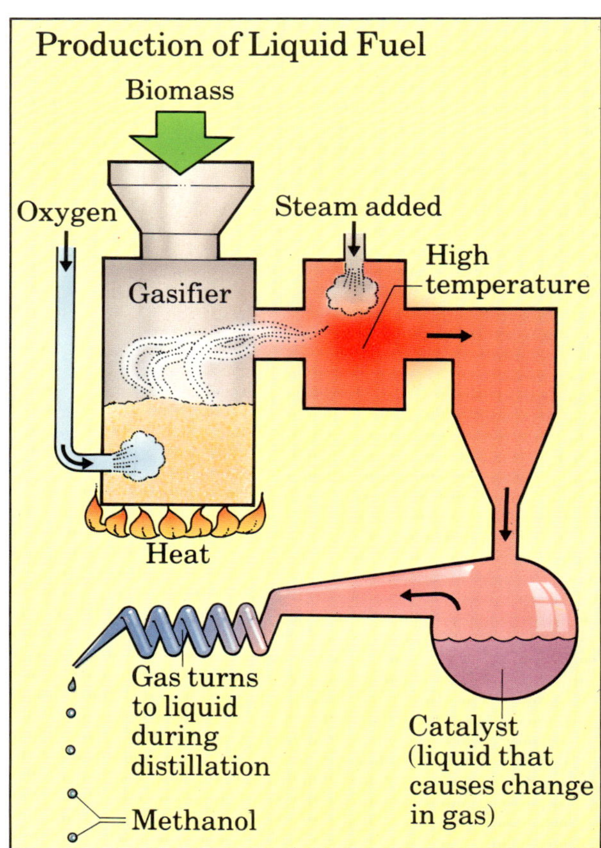

Above: Liquid fuel can be made from sugarcane, wood, or even seaweed.

The alcohol is added to gasoline. This mixture is called gasohol. In the U.S., about 30 percent of all gasoline sold has some alcohol added to it.

A crop of sugarcane in Martinique in the Caribbean. The sugarcane can be used to make fuel for cars.

But it is in Brazil that the greatest efforts have been made to produce alcohol for fuel. Sugarcane is grown as a fuel crop there. A factory at São Paulo makes about 320,000 gallons (1.2 million L) of alcohol each day.

However, alcohol is an expensive fuel to make, and if it is to be considered as an efficient and useful energy source, we must find ways of reducing the cost of making it.

In addition to Brazil and the U.S., gasohol is produced in Africa as a fuel for cars, in Malawi and Zimbabwe. Gasohol is used in many parts of Africa and is as common as gasoline at most gas stations there.

BIOENERGY IN ACTION

Crops that have a high oil content can also supply liquid fuel for diesel engines. These include soybeans, coconuts, and sunflowers. These are crushed to squeeze out their oil content. This oil can then be used, without any further processing, in diesel engines to power trucks, tractors, and electric generators. Much work still needs to be done to improve the efficiency of biofuels

Although biofuels have always been used on a small scale, as shown here, large-scale projects are now being built.

This factory in Brazil produces alcohol from sugarcane. The alcohol is used instead of gasoline to fuel cars.

and to reduce the cost of their production. But there are many biofuels already in use on a large scale. A company in Puerto Rico has built the largest digester in the world for producing biogas. This digester treats about 31,000 pounds (14,000 kg) of factory waste and produces 55,600 cubic yards (42,500 cu m) of gas each

This picture shows a biogas digester in the background and a storage tank in the foreground.

day. The gas is used in boilers in the factory and supplies about 40 percent of the company's energy.

The company is building a second digester. Not only will it be able to supply all its own energy needs, but it will also have a surplus of fuel to sell to other people.

A Welsh company uses a smaller but equally efficient digester. The digester there uses a by-product of dairy foods to produce biogas. Since building the digester, the company has saved thousands of dollars in energy costs each year.

In addition, after the waste from the digester has been processed, it is clean enough to discharge into a nearby river without causing dangerous pollution. Not only is this digester saving the company large sums of money, but it is friendly to the environment, too.

Sometimes, landfill sites are not available for the disposal of garbage. Often, however, this garbage can be burned to heat boilers. In Tennessee, a garbage-fueled power plant burns about 100 tons of waste each day. The heat generated is used to produce steam, which powers a turbine to produce electricity.

Despite the chance that burning gas may release poisonous materials into the atmosphere, our dependence on other treatments of biomass for energy will increase as the amount of fossil fuel decreases.

A number of poorer countries have created an organization, called the Biomass Users Network, to research ways of making biofuels from a variety of crops. They see these crops as a way to protect the environment and make use of land on which food crops will not grow.

As a natural source of alternative energy, bioenergy has been used for centuries, and will continue to be a reliable, clean, and safe fuel.

Household waste can be used to provide power in homes.

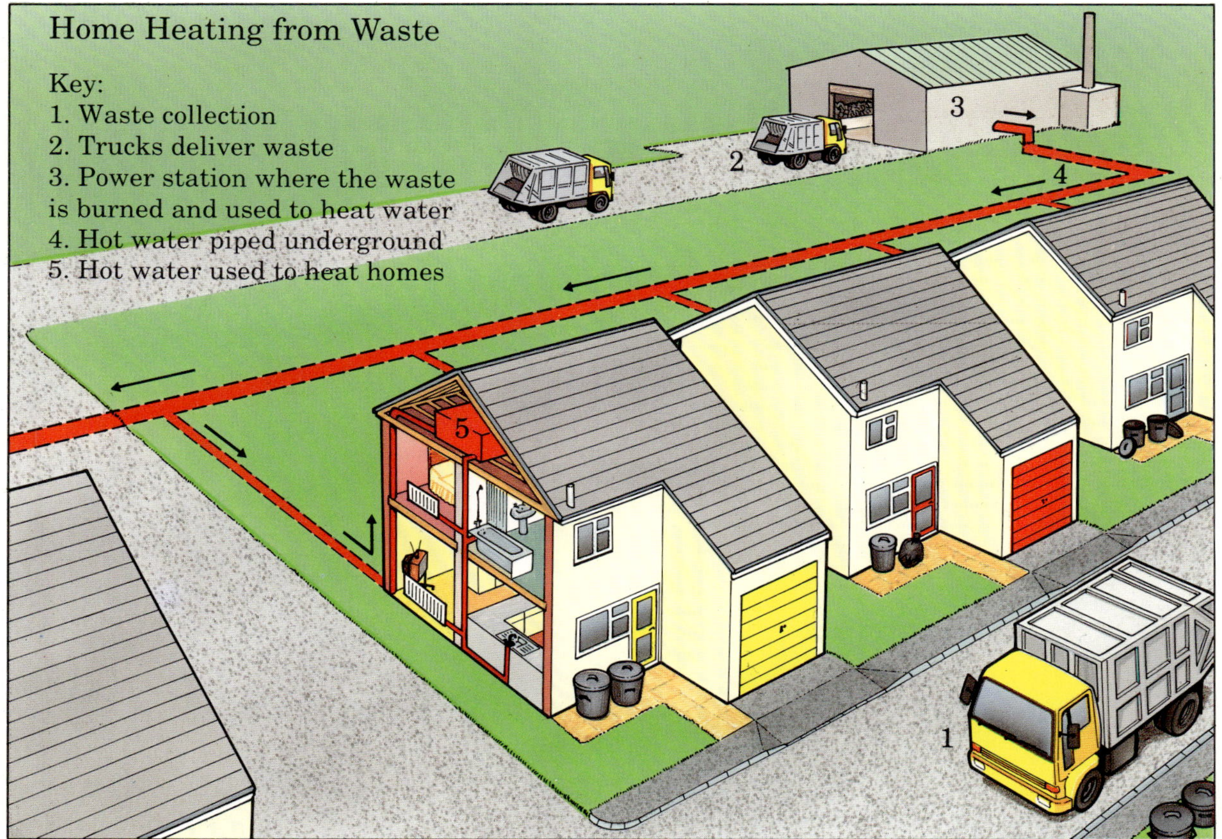

PROJECT

You will need:

- 2 tablespoons of dried yeast
- 2 tablespoons of sugar
- A balloon
- A small plastic soda bottle
- A plastic thermometer
- Some warm water

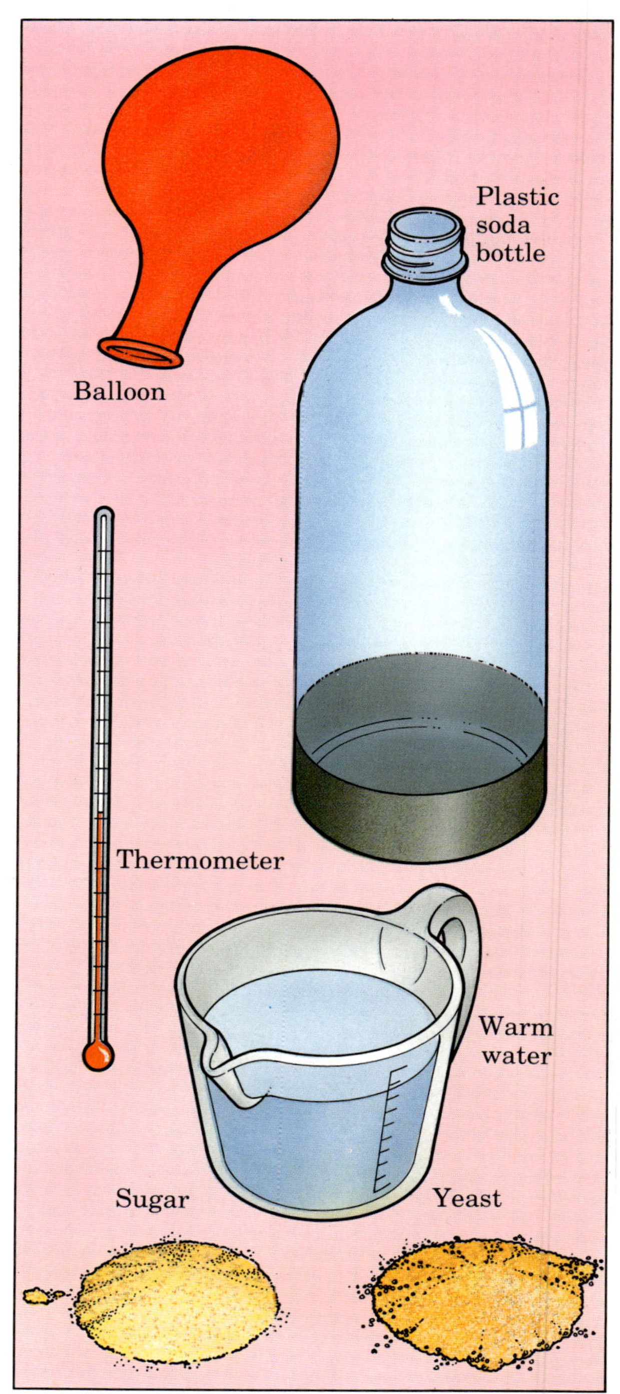

How to build your own biogas storage tank:

1. Pour the dried yeast and the sugar into the plastic bottle.

2. Pour in the warm water. Water from a faucet will be as warm as you need.

3. Cover the top of the bottle with your hand and shake it as hard as you can.

4. Put the balloon over the top of the bottle. If you leave it for an hour, the balloon will begin to fill up with gas.

5. Try the same experiment with water of different temperatures. Use the thermometer to measure the temperature of the water. Which fills the balloon most quickly — cold, hot, or warm water?

The balloon on top of the bottle will fill up in the same way that a biogas storage tank does.

Note:

The balloon fills up with gas in the same way that a storage tank for biogas does. The thing that makes the gas is the yeast. The yeast eats the sugar and emits gas as a result. Do you remember the biogas digester that had waste poured into it? The waste was eaten by the gas-producing bacteria. This project shows a similar process. From the results of your comparison of different temperatures, can you guess at what temperatures the bacteria would produce gas most quickly?

Glossary

Acid rain: Rain formed by pollution in the air combining with water vapor in clouds. It kills trees and wildlife, and, in time, will even eat away stone.

Bioenergy: The energy of living things; energy that is obtained from biofuel.

Biofuel: Any fuel obtained from biomass (plants).

Biogas: Biofuel in the form of gas. Biogas can be produced from materials such as roasted wood, sewage, and waste.

Biomass: Plants and parts of plants.

Carbohydrates: Quick-energy foods, such as sugar, made largely of carbon and water.

Carnivore: An animal, such as a wolf, dog, or cat, that eats other animals.

Charcoal: A fuel produced by burning wood with a restricted air supply.

Combustion: The process of burning. Combustion produces energy in the form of heat and light.

Digester: A tank in which organic wastes are stored to produce methane.

Efficient: Working well; producing results with little waste or loss of energy.

Fermentation: The conversion of sugar to alcohol by the action of yeast.

Flammable: Able to catch fire and burn easily.

Fossil fuels: Energy sources, such as coal, oil, and natural gas, formed from the remains of plants and animals that lived millions of years ago.

Gasification: Producing biogas by heating wood under pressure.

Gasohol: A mixture of gasoline and alcohol.

Greenhouse effect: The warming of the Earth due to gases in the atmosphere that trap the Sun's heat.

Greenhouse gases: Gases, such as carbon dioxide or methane, that trap the Sun's heat.

Herbivore: An animal, such as a cow or mouse, that eats plants.

Methane: A flammable gas produced by the decaying of organic matter.

Organic: Derived from living matter, whether animal or plant.

Pollution: Anything that dirties our environment, whether gas (air pollution), liquid (water pollution), or solid (ground pollution).

Smelt: To heat rock in order to remove metal from it.

Books to Read

Energy. Illa Podendorf (Childrens Press)
Energy at Work. John Satchwell (Lothrop, Lee & Shepard)
Fuel and Energy. Herta S. Breiter (Raintree)
Small Energy Sources: Choices That Work. Augusta Goldin (Harcourt Brace Jovanovich)
Understanding Energy. Neil Ardley (Silver Burdett)
Wonders of Energy. David Adler (Troll Associates)
Wood and Coal. (Silver Burdett)
Young Scientists Explore: An Encyclopedia of Energy Activities. Jerry DeBruin (Good Apple)

Places to Write

These groups can help you find out more about bioenergy and alternative energy in general. When you write, be sure to ask specific questions, and always include your full name, address, and age.

In the United States:

Conservation and Renewable Energy Inquiry and Referral Service
P.O. Box 8900
Silver Spring, MD 20907

Biomass Energy Research Association
777 North Capitol Street NE
Washington, DC 20002-4226

In Canada:

Biomass Energy Institute
1329 Niakwa Road, East
Winnipeg, Manitoba R2J 3T4

Canadian Wood Energy Institute
P.O. Box 32509
9665 Bayview Avenue
Richmond Hill, Ontario L4C 0A2

Efficiency and Alternative Energy Technology Board
Department of Energy, Mines, and Resources
580 Booth Street, 7th Floor
Ottawa, Ontario K1A 0E4

Index

A **boldface** number means that the entry is illustrated on that page.